DEEP GLIMPSES

REMEMBERING COMMUNION

Three Components of Remembering Christ to
Deepen the Expression of Communion

P.J. ALLAN

Published by Deep Glimpses
www.deepglimpses.com

Print ISBN: 979-8-9928260-0-5
Ebook ISBN: 979-8-9928260-1-2

Printed in the United States

CONTENTS

PREFACE

A Base Belief

I wish you could have known my godfather. He was in my life since birth and was a major contributor to my childhood. He was a bright spot in an otherwise dark, dismal, and gloomy family culture. He was the most kind, meek, generous, hospitable, trustworthy, faithful, and joyful man I have ever known. I called him Uncle Eddy although he was not a blood relative. I believe he was a coworker with my parents and a family friend. He would babysit my sister and me when my parents went out on a date. It was at his home where I had my first glance at a color TV when we were watching *The Wizard of Oz*. I'll never forget when the screen turned from black and white to the magical, colorful Land of Oz.

My Uncle Eddy was responsible for making our Christmases full of gifts beyond our dreams, and you could see the joy on his face knowing he made our holidays wonderful. He was never married and lived in a very humble three-room upstairs rented apartment the next street over. He was a hardworking man with a slight infirmity—his right thumb was missing from an industrial accident before I was born.

One day while we were all sitting around, I asked him why he wasn't married. I was probably around eight years old, and everybody else around us was married. So he began to tell his story about how he always thought he was supposed to be a priest. He attended seminary and began pursuing his calling. It was during that time he lost his thumb. He was then rejected from the seminary because in order to hold the bread during Communion in the required fashion, he would have to use both thumbs. True story! They would not allow him to continue pursuing his calling because he was missing a thumb. I remember, even at a young age, feeling the injustice of this whole thing. It seemed ridiculous to me—why couldn't he just use the other thumb?

That was really the first time I started looking at religion differently. Raising the bar to what qualified or disqualified someone to partake or administer Communion made a broader divide between those approved and those disapproved. I started asking more questions and looking carefully into this mysterious realm of the clergy. What made them different from the rest of us? This led me to see serious inconsistencies and, from my sincere inquiries, many hypocrisies. According to Scripture, all true believers in Christ are priests.

> *Coming to Him as to a living stone, rejected indeed by men, but chosen by God and precious, you also, as living stones, are being built up a spiritual house, a holy priesthood, to offer up spiritual sacrifices acceptable to God through Jesus Christ. Therefore it is also contained in the Scripture,*

"Behold, I lay in Zion a chief cornerstone, elect, precious, and he who believes on Him will by no means be put to shame."

Therefore, to you who believe, He is precious; but to those who are disobedient,

"The stone which the builders rejected has become the chief cornerstone," and "A stone of stumbling and a rock of offense."

They stumble, being disobedient to the word, to which they also were appointed. But you are a chosen generation, a royal priesthood, a holy nation, His own special people, that you may proclaim the praises of Him who called you out of darkness into His marvelous light; who once were not a people but are now the people of God, who had not obtained mercy but now have obtained mercy.

—1 Peter 2:4–10

I'd like to dedicate this booklet in loving memory to my Uncle Eddy, who, though physically disqualified from an official spiritual service, actually became more spiritually fruitful in my life and the lives of many others with a true operation in the fruit of the Spirit.

INTRODUCTION

Then He took the cup, and gave thanks, and said, "Take this and divide it among yourselves; for I say to you, I will not drink of the fruit of the vine until the kingdom of God comes." And He took bread, gave thanks and broke it, and gave it to them, saying, "This is My body which is given for you; do this in remembrance of Me."

—Luke 22:17-19*

What do you remember when you partake of Communion? Do you remember Jesus died at Calvary 2000 years ago? Do you remember your salvation? What *should* we be remembering?

On one occasion, my wife and I decided to have Communion together alone in our home. We set a time a few days ahead, and I began to pray and prepare for it. I asked myself the above questions. And knowing this time would be just for my wife and me, I realized the connection between marriage and Communion. There are things you can remember about your marriage, and they tie directly into what you can remember

*emphasis added

about Christ and your salvation. When we had our Communion time, it lasted close to an hour and a half. To our delight, we were digging into new wells of communion that enriched our faith and our marriage. This time of "remembering" deepened our relationship in ways we had yet to discover.

In direct comparison, what we are going to study in this booklet are three aspects of "remembering" that apply both to marriage and our covenant with Christ Jesus. Now, you don't have to be married to understand this comparison. The truths shared here will apply perfectly in every individual who desires a closer communion with Jesus. In fact, the apostle Paul was never married and actually wrote the principles we're sharing here. This is intended to provide a workbook or outline for small groups to interact with one another and with the Lord while sharing in the Lord's Supper or Communion together.

*This is not a book to read for knowledge only,
although you could learn something, but rather
to read for application and interaction.*

I will highlight some of my suggestions for how to best facilitate this interaction in the closing chapters once we understand the principles.

Can Our Current Church Structure Do Better?

After pastoring for thirty-three years, I can look back and clearly see three prominent expressions of my ministry that always left me with a sense of being incomplete or at least not having their full potential expressed. This doesn't mean they weren't valid, but they were just partial and not fully developed.

The first expression of ministry that left me with a sense of incompleteness was that we never seemed to have enough money to help everyone who needed financial aid. I always believed the expression of charity should be a strong aspect of the Body of Christ.

> *They desired only that we should <u>remember the poor</u>,*
> *the very thing which I also was eager to do.*
>
> *—Galatians 2:10**

> *He who has pity on <u>the poor</u> lends to the LORD,*
> *And He will pay back what he has given.*
>
> *—Proverbs 19:17**

I remember saying to our financial administrator, "Never let our gate of charity squeak." We did have a monthly budgeted allotment allocated to benevolence, but that would be quickly exhausted each and every month. Actually, in honest

---

*emphasis added

retrospect, it wasn't that we didn't have enough resources, but rather, regrettably, because of the traditional structure we operated under, the competing budget items redirected our funds more toward maintenance than mission.

The second expression of ministry that left me with a sense of incompleteness was not everyone who prayed for healing was, in fact, healed. Now, of course, we all understand that our personal preferences would always lean into what we believe would be the best outcome, at least from our perspective— that everyone gets healed. God is sovereign, and He rules and over-rules. We can all agree that the actual power to heal is exclusively in His hand alone. So we can easily settle into a resolve that says, "His will be done." And I, for the most part, gladly align with that conclusion, though I still see a tremendous operational divide between the ability to freely follow the leading of the Holy Spirit as it relates to the gift of healings referred to in 1 Corinthians 12:7–9:

> But the manifestation of the Spirit is given to each one for the profit of all: for to one is given the word of wisdom through the Spirit, to another the word of knowledge through the same Spirit, to another faith by the same Spirit, to another gifts of healings by the same Spirit.*

In many instances, we seemed to be led to pray for the sick by following the unction of a doctrinal belief or a

*emphasis added

congregational culture expectation instead of an authentic, independent leading of the Holy Spirit, which I believe would yield a completely different outcome. What I'm suggesting here is that if the Bible states that it is the Holy Spirit who disperses His gifts for the profit of all, shouldn't we then be primarily led by His unction to do so? Many times leaders initiate an effort to pray for healings based on motives other than a pure and simple leading of the Holy Spirit, i.e., congregational expectations, doctrinal declarations, or desperate cultural demands.

The third expression was that no matter what types of programs were established to bring people together and forge relationships, they often didn't seem to work very well. Don't get me wrong—we had home groups, volunteer appreciation dinners, men's breakfasts, ladies' Bible studies, a variety of small groups . . . you name it. As a result, there were relationships developed, and some lasted through time and are still intact today. But I have to distinguish between personal relationships and the actual strengthening of our bond in Christ for the edification of His body and its growth and influence in this world.

It seems that even though Christ was the
initial focal point of our gatherings, the
subordinate interests actually took on priority
focus and became a distraction from Him.

This includes the consecration and sanctification aspects of growing into members of His body.

We learned more than we grew,
conformed more than transformed.

Even in Bible studies, there evolved an unspoken leaning on the academic level instead of living it out in application. We learned more than we grew, conformed more than transformed. For example, we had a motorcycle ministry intending to reach out to the subculture of the motorcycle community. But instead of turning bikers into Christians, it turned Christians into bikers. Guys bought bikes and got tattoos that never should have. They endangered themselves and others around them. That's just one example of the tendency of groups to lose sight of priority in Christ and get tangled in the subordinate interest rallying them or, in other words, "The tail was wagging the dog." All the components were there, but the priority had shifted. What formed were circles or siloes of limited inclusion or, worse, groups that divided and isolated themselves. They seemed to ring shallow, superficial, and only scratched the surface of what was a higher calling to gather *in Christ*. It's a subtle and gradual shift almost unnoticeable. It's a resting into a comfort, a control that limits growing deeper, and became the status quo.

It's what many say about church in our day: "The church is like an ocean two inches deep." In most church settings, there are usually only a few people who have a dominant influence in the room, while everyone else is simply a spectator or at best supportive, but subdued, responders. I do not blame individual leaders for this, but rather the adopted structures or systems we've inherited from centuries of tradition.

The most blatant manifestation of this void for me was found in our times of Communion. It was supposedly the most intimate time with the Lord and with one another, yet it was seemingly compressed and hurried—encapsulated into passing the elements that were intended to be a manifestation of the most holy expression, "showing forth the Lord's death till He comes" and our strongest connection to our Christian faith and shared bond with Him and one another. The symbol of the cross is significant in its structure. It has a vertical beam with a horizontal beam. I believe the manifestation of this as expressed in Communion should include both a vertical connection with Christ as well as a horizontal connection with fellow members of His body.

The only connecting or interaction among participators in the traditional sense of the Communion service is the balancing act of passing the elements down the row without dropping or spilling anything. Listen, my intention here is not to stand at a distance and throw rocks at the stained-glass windows but rather to offer a possible solution or starting point to begin deepening our connection with Christ and one another. By focusing and developing a stronger emphasis on the importance of the Lord's Table, we can begin exploring the depths this living example given by the Lord Himself can bring to our times of gathering.

The Need for Deeper Expression of Communion

The purpose for this booklet is to provide a varied system or structure alternative that can facilitate a deeper expression of Communion. This booklet is not meant to be exhaustive in an apologetic way but rather a simple guideline or instructional manual so that small, individual groups of believers can experience a deeper communion with Christ and with one another. I always did and continue to have a strong desire to see the body of Christ unite, as depicted in Scripture:

> And they continued steadfastly in the apostles' doctrine and fellowship, in the breaking of bread, and in prayers. Then fear came upon every soul, and many wonders and signs were done through the apostles.

*emphasis added

Now all who believed were together, and had all things in common, and sold their possessions and goods, and divided them among all, as anyone had need. So continuing daily with one accord in the temple, and break-ing bread from house to house, they ate their food with gladness and simplicity of heart, praising God and having favor with all the people. And the Lord added to the church daily those who were being saved.

—Acts 2:42–47*

Obviously, they were living in a different socioeconomic reality, but the Spirit that connected them should be the same in our day. Their gatherings were simple yet profound and powerful. And in Ephesians we read:

And He Himself gave some to be apostles, some proph-ets, some evangelists, and some pastors and teachers, for the equipping of the saints for the work of ministry, for the edifying of the body of Christ, till we all come to the unity of the faith and of the knowledge of the Son of God, to a perfect man, to the measure of the stat-ure of the fullness of Christ; that we should no longer be children, tossed to and fro and carried about with every wind of doctrine, by the trickery of men, in the cunning craftiness of deceitful plotting, but, speaking the truth in love, may grow up in all things into Him

*emphasis added

13

who is the head—Christ—<u>from whom the whole body,</u>
<u>*joined and knit together by what every joint supplies,*</u>
<u>*according to the effective working by which every part*</u>
<u>*does its share,*</u> *causes growth of the body for the edify-*
ing of itself in love.

—Ephesians 4:11-16*

This scripture definitely points to the need for individual believers to rise above the posture of a spectator or observer to an activated, engaged, and contributing member in the work of the ministry as well as helping in the edification and growth of the body of Christ in love.

*For I received from the Lord that which I also delivered to you: that the Lord Jesus on the same night in which He was betrayed took bread; and when He had given thanks, He broke it and said, "Take, eat; this is My body which is broken for you; do this in **remembrance of Me.**" In the same **manner** He also took the cup after supper, saying, "This cup is the new covenant in My blood. This do, as often as you drink it, in **remembrance of Me.**" For as often as you eat this bread and drink this cup, you proclaim the Lord's death till He comes.*

—1 Corinthians 11:23–26*

*emphasis added

Now here's where we are called to examine ourselves and the "manner" in which we participate.

> *Therefore whoever eats this bread or drinks this cup of the Lord in an* **unworthy manner** *will be guilty of the body and blood of the Lord. But let a man* examine himself, *and so let him eat of the bread and drink of the cup.* [29] *For he who eats and drinks in an* **unworthy manner** *eats and* drinks judgment to himself, not discerning the Lord's body. **For this reason many are weak and sick among you, and many sleep.** *For if we would judge ourselves, we would not be judged. But when we are judged, we are chastened by the Lord, that we may not be condemned with the world. Therefore, my brethren, when you come together to eat, wait for one another. But if anyone is hungry, let him eat at home, lest you come together for judgment.*
>
> —*1 Corinthians 11:27-34**

It seems the church in Corinth had a lack of etiquette regarding the Spirit by which this essential expression took place. It sounds like a whole meal was included in their time together, and then the cup and bread were shared ceremonially, which is a good pattern to follow. The times we personally

---

*emphasis added

invited people over, it was for dinner and Communion. But in verse 29, we read that eating and drinking in an UNWORTHY MANNER can consequentially bring judgment with it, and the focal point of this judgment is *not discerning the Lord's body.* The consequences for this lack of discernment are some became weak or sick and many slept. In many other texts, this reference to sleep means they died.

When Paul encountered Christ on the road to Damascus, there was an insightful exchange that makes a connection to Christ and His people.

> As he journeyed he came near Damascus, and suddenly a light shone around him from heaven. Then he fell to the ground, and heard a voice saying to him, "Saul, Saul, why are **you persecuting Me**?"
>
> And he said, "Who are You, Lord?"
>
> Then the Lord said, "**I am Jesus, whom you are persecuting**. It is hard for you to kick against the goads."
>
> —Acts 9:3–5*

According to this exchange, if Paul persecuted the Church, the people who were redeemed by Christ, then Paul was directly persecuting Jesus Himself. Do you think that same connection is what we are reading in 1 Corinthians 11:29 . . . *not discerning the Lord's body?*

*emphasis added

*For I say, through the grace given to me, to everyone
who is among you, not to think of himself more highly
than he ought to think, but to think soberly, as God has
dealt to each one a measure of faith. <u>For as we have
many members in one body, but all the members do
not have the same function, so we, being many, are
one body in Christ, and individually members of one
another.</u>*

—*Romans 12:3-5**

It seems discerning the Lord's body has a two-pronged focus. First is recognizing that Christ is the head of the body, but we must also recognize our individual contribution as being members connected to Him and each other that actually produces a "worthy manner" in which to participate in Communion.

The scripture is also clear that by "not discerning the Lord's body," it creates a void, an emptiness that allows for negative consequences such as being weak, sick, and sleeping (death). Just reasoning this out, it seems to be saying that when we recognize and discern the Lord's body, we become a part with Jesus, and that solid, substantial intimacy brings power and life that would defer being weak, sick, or sleeping. I'm sorry to say, but in the traditional sense, many seem to totally miss discerning the Lord's body. Oftentimes, the focus is on the elements, which are mere symbols of the essence Christ Jesus died to provide for us. But the priority must allow a focus on our shared salvation and on the oneness we have in Him.

*emphasis added

Comparing Christ and His Church to Marriage

There are many scriptures that connect Christ with His Church, drawing a comparison as with a husband and wife.

Paul writes to the Corinthians in 2 Corinthians 11:2:

> For I am jealous over you with godly jealousy. For I have bethrothed you <u>to one husband</u>, that I may present you as a <u>chaste virgin to Christ</u>.*

Also written by Paul in Ephesians 5:23–27, we read:

> For the husband is the head of the wife, even as Christ is the head of the church; and He is the Savior of the body. Therefore, just as the church is subject to Christ, so let the wives be to their own husbands in everything. Husbands, love your wives, just as Christ also loved the church, and gave Himself for her, that He might sanctify and cleanse her with the washing of water by the word, that He might present her to Himself a glorious church, not having spot or wrinkle or any such thing, but that she should be holy and without blemish.

Another aspect to consider is that our salvation is based upon a covenant just as is marriage. In fact, Jesus states that the Lord's Table is the seal of this covenant salvation.

*emphasis added

And as they were eating, Jesus took bread, blessed and broke it, and gave it to the disciples and said, "Take, eat; this is My body."

Then He took the cup, and gave thanks, and gave it to them, saying, "Drink from it, all of you. For this is <u>My blood of the new covenant</u>, which is shed for many for the remission of sins. But I say to you, I will not drink of this fruit of the vine from now on until that day when I drink it new with you in My Father's kingdom."

—Matthew 26:26–29*

The amazing thing about this simple expression of the Lord's Table is that we will share in it with Jesus Christ Himself in His Father's kingdom. This wonderful table where we gather in remembrance will one day come into its full manifestation as the believers from every generation, tongue, tribe, and nation are for the first time all assembled together in one place with Christ Himself—then He lifts His cup! And we will, with joyful shouts of praise, commemorate the sacrifice that brought us all together. Can you imagine? What a time that will be! GLORY! The wedding supper of the Lamb! This is all the more reason for us to get this right or at least closer to a deep meaningful and spiritual connection.

*emphasis added

———ⱳⱳ∘∘ᴄᴛᴏᴏᴛ∘ᴏᴏⱳⱳ———

A covenant is different from a contract;
a covenant is made with a price or sacrifice.

———ⱳⱳ∘ᴄᴛᴏ∘ᴄᴛᴏᴏ∘ᴏⱳⱳ———

The essence here is that a covenant is different from a contract. A covenant is made with a price or sacrifice. (Look again at the above verse in Matthew: *For this is <u>My blood of the new covenant</u>, which is shed for many for the remission of sins.** People miss this most important meaning as they approach marriage in our day. It seems the whole focus is on the external components of the wedding—the dress, the flowers, the party, the gimmicks, outdoing their friend's wedding, etc. In fact, after doing many, many weddings, I was often surprised how the actual ceremony of the marriage was less attended than the receptions. It is, after all, the intention of the guests to be witnesses of the vows made to each other at the altar.

It definitely speaks to the shift in our culture from spiritual to material, from sacrifice to pleasure, from delayed gratification to instant gratification. They are missing the bigger picture that the wedding is just the beginning of a marriage and not the all that ends all. People who approach marriage with this shallow perspective usually suffer the consequences in the long run. Once the wedding is over, they go back to pursuing their careers, sports, and entertainment and mount the marriage license up next to the deer head. "There, that's done; now we can get on with our lives." The wedding is not the end by far; it's only the beginning.

In light of this truth, let's attempt to lay down a parallel track … picture a train track with two parallel rails. The first rail is between a husband and wife in marriage, and the second rail is between Christ and His Church (His bride).

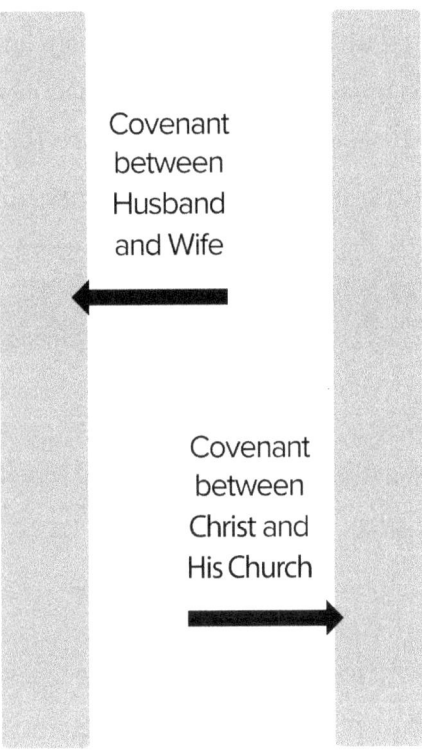

Covenant between Husband and Wife

Covenant between Christ and His Church

Both relational connections are bound by a covenant. Both involve a sacrifice in the making of that covenant work. Of course, the sacrifice that Christ made was at Calvary's cross where He laid down His life and shed His blood as the means to ransom His bride from sin, death, and hell. I believe that the intrinsic aspects of marriage should be bound by the same level of sacrifice.

Husbands, love your wives, just as Christ also loved the church and gave Himself for her, that He might sanctify and cleanse her with the washing of water by the word, that He might present her to Himself a glorious church, not having spot or wrinkle or any such thing, but that she should be holy and without blemish. So husbands ought to love their own wives as their own bodies; he who loves his wife loves himself. For no one ever hated his own flesh, but nourishes and cherishes it, just as the Lord does the church.

—Ephesians 5:25-29

There is a reason that traditional marriages took place on an altar—an altar is a place of sacrifice.

Back when sacrifices were made by the priests, people would bring their sheep or pigeons to the temple, and the priest would slay that offering on the altar and present it to the Lord. When I would do premarital counseling with couples, I would take my letter opener and hold it like a dagger, saying that two 'I's approach the altar, but one 'us' walks away. The *I, me,* and *mine* die at the altar, and the *us, we,* and *our* leave to build a marriage and begin the journey to become one flesh. I would then encourage the couple to speak into their marriage by using these plural words. Staying away from words like *mine, I,* and *me* and using words like *our, we,* and *us* helps to build and contribute to constructing a marriage. In fact, if they were to have children, I would tell them that they would be little us's and little "we's" ... my wife calls them "little we wees." When you consider the words of Christ spoken in Matthew 18 and apply it to marriage, you can see the power accessible there in its core.

> For where two or three are gathered together in My name, I am there in the midst of them.
>
> —Matthew 18:20

I believe that is the reason marriages are under such direct attack. There is intrinsic power when a husband and wife at their core are gathered together in His name. He is in their midst. What access, what power in agreement! I believe this same intrinsic power is available to all those who are in true communion with Christ and each other.

In the next section, we will go deeper into a practice of the Lord's Table that will lead to a more meaningful expression of Communion in the hope that it reflects the intimacy and significance of this call to remembrance.

How to Put This Book into Practice

L et's first consider the components of remembering as they relate to a marriage. Then, we will apply that same focus as it relates to Christ and our salvation. Using the illustration mentioned earlier, the two lines represent Christ/ His Church and marriage. We will start laying horizontal bridges that tie the similar components together. We start by remembering where it all began.

First: Remember Your Wedding— Remember Your Salvation

Let's say a married couple was celebrating their anniversary. They go out for a nice dinner, someplace romantic, with candlelight and the right ambiance, and the wife says, "Remember our wedding?"

A wedding is a historical event that happened some time ago but can still be remembered. It had specific aspects and experiences that made it unique. The wedding changed your life. From that moment on, you were no longer single, but your life became entwined with another person for better or worse. And just like you can remember a wedding, so, too, you can remember when your life in Christ began. Only now you're sitting at the Lord's Table and are asked to remember when you accepted Christ's sacrifice for your sins.

What were the circumstances in your life that brought you to Jesus? What did it feel like to be forgiven of your sins? When did you make that decision that changed everything for you?

*Just like you can remember a wedding, so, too, you
can remember when your life in Christ began.*

You should be able to remember when Jesus became real to you—even if you were raised in a Christian home and can't remember a time when Jesus wasn't a part of your life. There is still a moment when you embraced His love for you and gave permission for Him to become your Lord and Savior. There was a moment when you realized you were a sinner and needed to personally accept His sacrifice for your sins. There is that kind of remembrance for many as they approach the Communion table. We remember that Jesus died for our sins on Calvary, a historic event that happened years ago, but that moment still carries significance and meaning in our lives today. Another event that can be recalled on a timeline is when we took up our cross, counting ourselves dead to sin but alive to follow Christ. Some may consider their baptism as that time they surrendered their lives to Jesus.

> *Or do you not know that as many of us as were baptized into Christ Jesus were baptized into His death? Therefore we were buried with Him through baptism into death, that just as Christ was raised from the dead by the glory of the Father, even so we also should walk in newness of life.*
>
> *—Romans 6:3–4*

For I delivered to you first of all that which I also received: that Christ <u>died for our sins</u> according to the Scriptures, and that He was buried, and that He rose again the third day according to the Scriptures.

—1 Corinthians 15:3-4*

I beseech you therefore, brethren, by the mercies of God, that you present your <u>bodies a living sacrifice</u>, holy, acceptable to God, which is your reasonable service.

—Romans 12:1*

Therefore take heed to yourselves and to all the flock, among which the Holy Spirit has made you overseers, to shepherd the church of God which He purchased with His own blood.

—Acts 20:28

In Him you also trusted, after you heard the word of truth, the gospel of your salvation; in whom also, having believed, you were sealed with the Holy Spirit of promise.

—Ephesians 1:13

*emphasis added

Application: Remember Your Salvation

At this time, each person in your group would take turns sharing around the table their remembrance of when they first gave their life to Jesus Christ. When we say, "gave our lives," we mean the first time someone offered themselves as a living sacrifice, they died with Christ. Again, a wedding is when two individuals die to self and are joined as one plural identity. So share when you allowed Jesus to "purchase" you by the price of His shed blood. This is your *testimony*! This is a wonderful time to glorify the Lord.

Sometimes testimonies can be messy, so try to encourage participants to avoid all the gory details and instead focus on Jesus. You are beginning to open each other up to "holy ground." You are welcoming the testimony of Christ to become part of your gathering. This is a powerful time; in fact, John tells us that we overcome by the blood of the Lamb and the word of our testimony.

> *For whatever is born of God overcomes the world. And this is the victory that has overcome the world—our faith. Who is he who overcomes the world, but he who believes that Jesus is the Son of God?*
>
> —1 John 5:4–5

You are of God, little children, and have overcome them, because He who is in you is greater than he who is in the world. They are of the world.

—*1 John 4:4-5*

And they overcame him by the blood of the Lamb and by the word of their testimony, and they did not love their lives to the death.

—*Revelation 12:11*

We have actually practiced and experienced this outline for Communion many times and with many people, and we have been shocked by the fact that people who have known one another for years can be unaware of each other's salvation story. We once had Communion with a married couple, and during this time the wife began crying and saying she "never heard that before" regarding her husband's testimony.

Another thing to prepare for is that some may not know when they accepted Jesus. This can be awkward for them. But you can make the time you are having Communion together be their time when they formally and officially accepted Jesus into their hearts. Now we all have something more to celebrate in our Communion time! This may be their first real Communion.

Once everyone has shared, it's good to celebrate and thank the Lord for His great work in our salvation. Be careful not to focus too heavily on any one testimony but still thank God for the work He has done in all of us. After this time of praise and thanksgiving, you can move on to the second remembrance.

Second: Remember You're Married—
Remember You're a Christian

Many believe that having a wedding is all there is to being married, and as I've already stated, that could not be further from the truth. The wedding is merely an event where the marriage begins. Too many couples, after their wedding, just go on as before they were married, i.e., going out with their single friends, pursuing careers, hobbies, and entertainment with the same intensity as they did before they were married.

I recall one wedding I did where they each had a professional career and scheduled their wedding on a day when their calendars were open—NO RECEPTION, NO HONEYMOON. They planned to go right back to work. I strongly opposed their approach to this kind of wedding and said for them to allow their marriage to "interrupt" their lives.

Your life should radically change after you are married. You are no longer a *single*, self-serving individual but are now a *plural* entity. The "we" must become stronger than the "I" if you are ever to experience the full expression of being married. Once the honeymoon is over, as they say, it's easy to go back to pursuing self-interests, hobbies, old friends, or careers. That other person, however, is meant to become your most important focus and priority. It is so easy to slip back into a self-survival mode. The exact opposite is what's necessary for a marriage to grow.

The marriage is started at the altar, but it doesn't mean that the sacrifice is over.

Paul wrote in relation to his walk with Christ:

I affirm, by the boasting in you which I have in Christ Jesus our Lord, I die daily.

—*1 Corinthians 15:31**

I believe a sustaining marriage must have that same measure of self-sacrifice. This does not mean you walk around

*emphasis added

in martyrdom moping. There should be a strong substantial alternative deposited into your hearts that make the sacrifice of self a joy. You should be gaining something better and worth more than any selfish gratification. This is the difference between a marriage of two believers and a couple without Christ.

In the marriage without Christ, all they have is the love carried inside their own hearts—which is a limited resource. It can run thin at times and does not have the wherewithal to regain momentum. This stands in direct conflict with marriage in Christ. He stays in the center of both hearts, contributing motivation, inspiration, and resources to see the promise through. In other words, sometimes you may not want to be a good spouse for the person you're with, but you want to be a good spouse for the Lord, and your partner benefits from His supply.

> Two are better than one, because they have a good reward for their labor. For if they fall, one will lift up his companion. But woe to him who is alone when he falls, for he has no one to help him up. Again, if two lie down together, they will keep warm; but how can one be warm alone? Though one may be overpowered by another, two can withstand him. And a _threefold cord is not quickly broken_.
>
> —Ecclesiastes 4:9-12*

*emphasis added

If you were to take two strands of long hair and wrap them around each other then let go, the strands would simply unwind. But if you used three strands of hair and made a braid then let go, they would stay together. This is the strength of a three-stranded cord as referred in verse 12 above.

Imagine you've been married for a while, and your friends call and want to go out. These were the friends that would get you into trouble on occasion, and you can tell they're ready to party. You have a decision to make. That's when you hear a thought in your head say, "Remember, you're married." Now, I'm not saying that you can never go out with friends, but if you do, you're going out as a *married person*. As another example, maybe you have a coworker who is a bit flirtatious. It is very important in interactions with them to "remember you're married." Do you see how "remembering" affects your decisions in real time?

I believe remembering is more important
and significant, as it should affect
the way we live out our lives.

Just like being married affects our decisions and life choices, so should our being a Christian apply this same level of remembering into our walk with Christ. Sure, there was a time when you had a real, life-changing encounter with Jesus. But a lot has happened since then. Life happens, and there are many "in your face" realities. There are momentums and shifts, pressures and responsibilities. The world can at times "grab you by the throat" and put demands on your time and attention. This pressure can begin to bring out of you behavior or desires that pull you away from Christ. It is extremely important at those times to "remember you're a follower of Jesus."

This type of remembering ties directly into decision-making. The word *decision* comes from a base word meaning *incision*—to make a cut or separation. Remembering causes us to decide who and what we are, which, in turn, cuts off an option contrary to that identity. So when we make decisions in marriage and don't include our spouse in making those decisions together, we're actually cutting our spouse out of that choice and separating them from that part of our life.

Remembering causes us to decide who and what we are, which, in turn, cuts off an option contrary to that identity.

Now, I'm not talking about what to have for lunch or minor issues. I'm referring to life-defining decisions. An accumulating consequence to this practice is that you begin living separate lives together and the marriage is in a slow decline and can slip into a death spiral caused by the exclusion or neglect due to small cuts of decisions—literally "death by 1000 paper cuts."

If remembering you're married affects decisions and choices, so should your covenant with Christ. This is the second way we are remembering HIM. "Remember, you're a follower of Jesus Christ," and it should affect the choices you are making in real time today. Let that one sink in. When you are in a marriage or Christ-following relationship, and you make a decision opposite that relationship, you literally cut that person off or out of that part of your life. That's why remembering your relational identity is so important. Are you in a marriage? Are you in Christ?

Application: Remember You're a Christian

At this time, you would have your small group members go around the table and each one share how their current walk (discipleship) or progressive consecration and sanctification with Jesus is affecting decisions and choices in their lives. Don't let that verbiage confuse you. We are told that the Holy Spirit will lead and guide us into all truth. Walking in truth is how we change our lives. Also in Hebrews 12 we are told that the Lord corrects or chastens those He loves. What kind of correction have you had in your walk with the Lord? What things have been cut off because you follow Jesus? What positive actions are you doing because of Jesus being in your life? How are you living out your faith on a daily basis? Remember, you're a Christian!

Once each person has shared how they are remembering Christ through their everyday decisions, discipleship, and response to correction from the Lord, you will move on to the third remembrance.

Third: Remember You're in Communion— Remember You're in Intimacy

When I was in my early twenties, I worked at a factory where we made the long side guards for cars. You don't see them much anymore. They attached to the doors and to the front and rear quarter panels to protect the paint job from parking lot damage. The plastic was melted and then stretched out on a long conveyer belt. Once it extended to the desired length, a sharp hydraulic blade would engage to bevel cut the plastic. One day, a coworker running one of those lines went to reach for a scrap piece of plastic at unfortunately the exact time the blade was engaged. The blade cut off the top of his finger clean at the knuckle. I know, right? OUCH! They put the tip of the finger in ice and rushed him to the hospital. Fortunately, they were able to surgically attach his finger, although I'm not sure how well it functioned after that, but it was restored.

Now I want you to catch this: When his finger was severed, it was dis-membered, but after the surgery, it was re-membered, REMEMBER . . . to re-attach, to reconnect again.

I believe this example gives us insight into a major component of our communion with Christ. If we are each a part of His body, Communion is meant to re-member us with Him and with each other. We are to reconnect in Christ together. Hang on because this really opens up into some interesting insights.

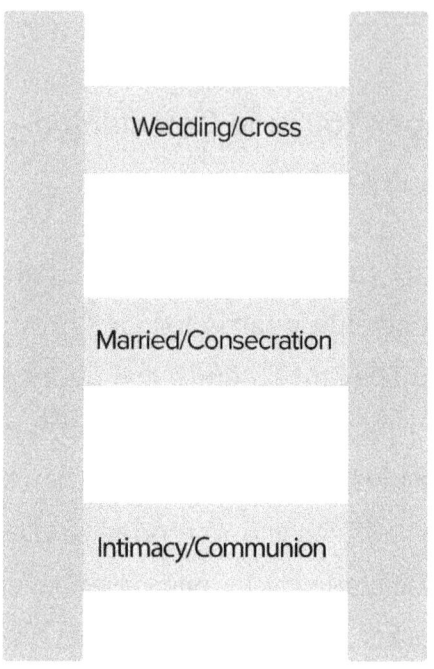

Our word *communion* comes from the Greek word *koinonia* (koy-nohn-ee'-ah).[1] *Koinonia* is defined as "partnership, participation, or (social) <u>intercourse</u>, communicate, communion, distribution, fellowship." If we are to continue in our parallel comparison between Communion and marriage, there is an obvious connection. But before we continue this any further, I think referring to Titus is appropriate here:

> To the pure all things are pure, but to those who are
> defiled and unbelieving nothing is pure; but even their
> mind and conscience are defiled.
>
> —Titus 1:15

---

[1] "Koinonia," *Strong's Concordance*, 2842.

As we have shared to this point, remembering a marriage relationship can be expressed in three ways: remembering your wedding, remembering you're married, and now, remembering through reconnecting in intimacy. There is an intended exclusive connection for consummating the marriage union where two become joined together as one. This specific union not only reinstates their priority and exclusivity toward each other but also makes their love increase toward one another and actually makes it possible for new life to enter their union. God made it that way! RE-MEMBER!

This idea of RE-MEMBERING has to be viewed through Scripture as Paul again sheds light onto how we are the body of Christ and each one a member that should connect to other members.

> For as the body is one and has many members, but all the members of that one body, being many, are one body, so also is Christ. For by one Spirit we were all baptized into one body—whether Jews or Greeks, whether slaves or free—and have all been made to drink into one Spirit. For in fact the body is not one member but many.
>
> If the foot should say, "Because I am not a hand, I am not of the body," is it therefore not of the body? And if the ear should say, "Because I am not an eye, I am not of the body," is it therefore not of the body? If the whole body were an eye, where would be the hearing? If the whole were hearing, where would be the smelling? But

now God has set the members, each one of them, in the body just as He pleased. And if they were all one member, where would the body be?

But now indeed there are many members, yet one body. And the eye cannot say to the hand, "I have no need of you"; nor again the head to the feet, "I have no need of you." No, much rather, those members of the body which seem to be weaker are necessary. And those members of the body which we think to be less honorable, on these we bestow greater honor; and our unpresentable parts have greater modesty, but our presentable parts have no need. But God composed the body, having given greater honor to that part which lacks it, that there should be no schism in the body, but that the members should have the same care for one another. And if one member suffers, all the members suffer with it; or if one member is honored, all the members rejoice with it. Now you are the body of Christ, and members individually.

—1 Corinthians 12:12–27

The above verses in 15 through 16 deal with self-exclusion—how individuals, through comparing themselves with other more prominent parts of the body, disqualify themselves. Verse 21 indicates how some parts may feel superior to others and disqualify those who appear to be less important. Communion is meant to illuminate these separating perspectives and bring us all equally to the feet of Jesus. Verses 25 through 26 sum this up nicely:

> *That there should be no schism in the body, but that the members should have the same care for one another. And if one member suffers, all the members suffer with it; or if one member is honored, all the members rejoice with it.*

Come union! Common union! Communion!

Communion is meant to bring us to a tenderness toward each other, a gentle appreciation and respect in Christ.

In Hebrews we read:

> *And let us consider one another in order to stir up love and good works, not forsaking the assembling of ourselves together, as is the manner of some, but exhorting one another, and so much the more as you see the Day approaching.*
>
> —*Hebrews 10:24-25*

This scripture speaks so much more than simply gathering in the same place for a time. Verse 24 instructs us to *consider one another* so we can *stir up love and good works.* That sounds like interaction to me. Also *exhort one another*—again, interaction.

Hebrews mentions "assembling," which is defined as "<u>a complete collection</u>, meeting (for worship) assembling (gathering) together."[2]

---

[2] "Assemble," *Strong's Concordance,* #1997.

Have you ever made a purchase of an item that needed to be assembled? A bicycle or perhaps a shelving unit? Somewhere on the package, you'll see the words "assembly required." So let me ask you, if you were to pour the content of that box into the center of the living room and say, "There ya go, all the pieces are there, so it's assembled," would you agree that it's assembled? I don't think so. Just because all the pieces are there does not mean that they are assembled into an object intended for a specific purpose.

Again, the definition seems to infer a "complete collection." Picture a puzzle: You can have all the pieces in the box, but the assembly actually takes place as one piece finds where it belongs and how it fits by its direct association with other specific pieces surrounding it. There is work involved with assembling something. The application and attention to how we fit together is important. To call a gathering an assembly, without working at how we all fit together, is just lazy (re-member).

Application: Remember You're in Intimacy

The goal of this time is to encounter Jesus as if for the first time, intimately. We come to Him confessing our desperate need for Him as if for the first time. Covenant! We forsake anything that has come between us, any distractions or hindrances to our walk with Him. This is a time of reflection and reverence, a time of prayer. Consecration! At this time, you would take a moment to allow individuals to pray and repent if need be. This time can open up to a place where someone may accept Jesus as Savior or rededicate their lives to Him. Be open to other spiritual needs that may surface. We are first "showing forth the Lord's death," then offering ourselves as living sacrifices. Intimacy!

> *Confess your trespasses to one another, and pray for one another, that you may be healed. The effective, fervent prayer of a righteous man avails much.*
>
> —*James 5:16*

A Word of Caution

In the previous two rememberings, you have been peeling back layers of personal protection. People have been sharing their testimonies and ways in which they are living out their faith. But you are about to take this to a new level of transparency and honesty. This must be approached reverently and with the understanding that this may open up deep hurts in others.

We learned how to cover ourselves from the beginning in the Garden. Adam and Eve used leaves to cover themselves before God, and we still do the same—not with leaves but with carefully arranged social and conversational protections, limiting or controlling conversations by intentionally avoiding certain subjects or topics.

These hidden areas of our hearts can begin to break down when we experience a fresh presence of the Lord. This could be accompanied by tears, anger, and wounds that haven't surfaced for a long time. Don't forget we are not just opening up to one another here but also before the Lord. We need to ask ourselves a serious question: Do we believe God wants us to grow beyond a candy-coated Christianity? One where whenever someone asks how you are doing, you always answer, "GREAT! PRAISE THE LORD"?

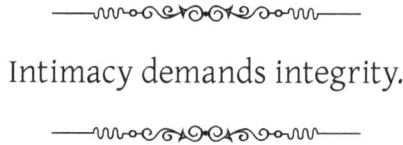

Intimacy demands integrity.

There are reasons intimacy breaks down in our walk with the Lord. Secret sins, broken relationships, personal loss, or trauma and faith crisis can all build a fortification around them. But I believe God is bigger than these. I believe that He desires deeper healing in us than just pretending the wounds aren't there and glossing over them with casual pleasantries.

This is why this third remembrance is to be a strong focus ON THE LORD. These issues are between them and God and not to be intercepted by us or the group. There should be a plan, if necessary, to refer someone with a deeper need to an elder or pastor in your community. On the other hand, if there is a supernatural breakthrough, guard and protect that investment of trust. You can have a sincere, spiritual breakthrough without going into details. Only share what can be kept in the love and trust of your group.

Distribution of the Elements

Once you have concluded the interaction in sharing the three types of remembering, it is now time to take the elements of the bread and the cup. You can begin by reading the scripture recording the act of breaking bread with Christ and His disciples found in Matthew 26:26–29, Mark 14:22–26, or Luke 22:14–22. You may also want to invite an elder or leader in the group to actually conduct the distribution of the elements. This could also be an honored patriarch/matriarch in a family context.

Select one of the scripture references and then read a partial part, i.e., "He took the bread," and then distribute the bread, pray, and partake together. You can do the same with the cup, reading the section, "He took the cup," passing the cup, and partaking together. Break up the reading so that it coincides with the distribution of the elements. Once all have received, close with prayer. Then just let each person share what they received from this experience.

On a Practical Note

Let me suggest an outline in planning and preparing to have Communion in your home with invited guests. We have had various settings and a varying number of participants from three to eleven. The best number I think is four. Now, you can have more, but just take into account the allotted time for sharing. The bigger the number, the longer it takes, and you never want to feel rushed. If you want to do this in a large group, just break out into smaller groups of three to four. Another thing is don't be afraid to invite someone who may not know the Lord. We had one instance with a family where one of their older sons couldn't remember when he gave his heart to the Lord. So we asked if it was something he wanted to do, he said yes, and our Communion service was his "locked in" date for his salvation!

We think it works best to have dinner together first. This is a nice time to break the ice and socialize. Then after dinner, bring the elements to the table and share what's about to happen. Pick someone to lead the discussion, preferably the host or hostess.

Another approach to consider is to allow each invited guest to read this booklet before your gathering, so they are both forewarned and open to the idea.

As far as the actual elements, it's safest to provide grape juice and matzo crackers and only a small amount of each. This should be separate from the dinner and more of a symbol than a substance.

You may also want to consider having some worship music playing in the background during your Communion time. A few songs I've found fitting:

- "To the Table" by Zach Williams
- "Remember Him" by Shane & David Belt
- "Come to the Table" by Sidewalk Prophets

IN CONCLUSION

Before Christ was crucified, He met privately with His disciples, and this would be their last time together. This was His last will and testament. He was setting a focal point and a practice that was intended to be the center of their gatherings from now on. In Revelation 19:10 we read:

> Then I fell down at his feet to worship him, but he said to me, "You must not do that! I am a fellow servant with you and your brothers who hold to the testimony of Jesus. Worship God." For the testimony of Jesus is the spirit of prophecy.*
>
> —Revelation 19:10

So what is the testimony of Jesus? I know what it means to testify "of" Jesus, but what was Jesus' testimony? I believe it is the bread and the cup. In these simple elements, we show forth the Lord's death until He comes (and there's the prophecy). When He took up the bread and blessed it, He was giving an illustrated sermon of what was about to happen at the cross.

---

*emphasis added

Then He broke the bread. We cannot miss what He was proph-
esying at this moment. When Jesus walked upon this earth,
He was God in flesh. The scripture says this in Colossians 2:9:

> *For in him the whole fullness of deity dwells bodily.*
> *—Colossians 2:9*

So what is being said here is that Jesus, in His body, held
the fullness of the Godhead bodily. The problem was His body
could only be at one place at a time. Remember Martha's
lament that if only Jesus was there, her brother wouldn't have
died? When Jesus was breaking the bread, He was showing that
He was about to franchise or be broken off into many, many
pieces. This one single body was about to be broken so that it
could multiply and be distributed through His disciples and
throughout the whole world. As He was distributing the pieces
of the broken bread to His disciples, in essence He was saying:
"Now, you're a part of me, and you're now a part of me, etc."
At the cross and the torturous whipping and beating prior to
the cross, His human body was being ripped to shreds. But
every laceration, each piercing of the skin, became an entry
point for us. Where the blood was shed is where the blood can
be received. Then, after the resurrection, Jesus ascended into
heaven. Remember what He said and look at it now through
hindsight:

> *I did not say these things to you from the beginning,*
> *because I was with you. But now I am going to Him*
> *who sent me, and none of you asks me, 'Where are you*

going?' But because I have said these things to you, sorrow has filled your heart. Nevertheless, I tell you the truth: <u>it is to your advantage that I go away</u>, for if I do not go away, the Helper will not come to you. But if I go, I will send him to you. And when he comes, he will convict the world concerning sin and righteousness and judgment: concerning sin, because they do not believe in me; concerning righteousness, because I go to the Father, and you will see me no longer; concerning judgment, because the ruler of this world is judged. I still have many things to say to you, but you cannot bear them now. When the Spirit of truth comes, he will guide you into all the truth, for he will not speak on his own authority, but whatever he hears he will speak, and he will declare to you the things <u>that are to come</u>. He will glorify me, for he will take what is mine and declare it to you. All that the Father has is mine; therefore I said that he will take what is mine and declare it to you.*

—John 16:4–15

Jesus is telling them that after He ascends, He will send the Holy Spirit, which was poured out on the day of Pentecost. The Holy Spirit filled the individual pieces of the broken body of Christ with power, so that now they, too, can be parts of the power of God in human form. Only Jesus had the fullness of

*emphasis added

49

God, but we hold a measure, a portion. And that's what brings power at the Lord's Table when we RE-MEMBER HIM! Our combined unity in Christ brings parts of Him together that may have never been united before . . . we are being assembled. Just picture the combined power of His body. He said, "Where two or more are gathered in my name, I am in the midst." I believe that we will begin to see healings and miracles at the Lord's Table. Because Jesus Christ is the same yesterday, today, and forever, and He is in our midst.

> When you come together, it is not the Lord's supper that you eat. For in eating, each one goes ahead with his own meal. One goes hungry, another gets drunk. What! Do you not have houses to eat and drink in? Or do you despise the church of God and humiliate those who have nothing? What shall I say to you? Shall I commend you in this? No, I will not.
>
> —1 Corinthians 11:20–22

> That is why many of you are weak and ill, and some have died.
>
> —1 Corinthians 11:30

Paul is here reproving the body of Christ in Corinth. He is exposing their fall from the established purpose of their meeting, the Lord's Table. In fact, verse 20 carries a strong inference that they are meant to be gathered to celebrate the Lord's Table, and they are missing it. Consequential to NOT sharing the Lord's Table correctly, he said some are weak and sick and sleep because they are missing the "worthy manner" in which the body of Christ is united and connecting at the Lord's Table. But what can we expect if we get this right? The opposite must be true as well. When we come to the Table of the Lord and correctly Re-Member Him, we should expect that we will be made strong, we will operate in health and healing, and we will be ALIVE, having life more abundant as He said He came to bring us.

The Macro Perspective

Alright, let's pan out and see if we can comprehend the bigger picture. At the time of His last supper with His disciples, Jesus instituted a simple practice that served as His last will and testament. I believe that blood-bought believers are meant to have this activity at the very center of their gatherings. The body of Christ is now being distributed into individuals who are purchased by the precious blood of Jesus and filled with the Holy Spirit's power. Throughout time, those being born again and Spirit filled, are partaking in this RE-MEMBERING process. The body of Christ has now been a part of every generation, of every tongue, in every tribe on the globe. In these, the end times, the Lord's Table is being emphasized with a new sense of intensity and purpose. Some say revival, others say reformation.

Now, let's look at a "blessed hope" many believe is soon coming and that would be the rapture or taking up of the body of Christ. Today, this is a controversial topic. Let me throw in my view. Many see the rapture as an escape from the wrath of God. I believe that is a part of it . . . but there is so much more. I am about to propose a hypothetical thesis or speculation in eschatology.

Then I saw in the right hand of him who was seated on the throne a scroll written within and on the back, sealed with seven seals. And I saw a mighty angel proclaiming with a loud voice, "Who is worthy to open the scroll and break its seals?" And no one in heaven or on earth or under the earth was able to open the scroll or to look into it, and I began to weep loudly because no one was found worthy to open the scroll or to look into it. And one of the elders said to me, "Weep no more; behold, the Lion of the tribe of Judah, the Root of David, has conquered, so that he can open the scroll and its seven seals." And between the throne and the four living creatures and among the elders I saw a Lamb standing, as though it had been slain, with seven horns and with seven eyes, which are the seven spirits of God sent out into all the earth. And he went and took the scroll from the right hand of him who was seated on the throne. And when he had taken the scroll, the four living creatures and the twenty-four elders fell down before the Lamb, each holding a harp, and golden bowls full of incense, which are the prayers of the saints. And they sang a new song, saying,

"Worthy are you to take the scroll and to open its seals, for you were slain, and by your blood you ransomed people for God from every tribe and language and people and nation, and you have made them a kingdom and priests to our God, and they shall reign on the earth."

Then I looked, and I heard around the throne and the living creatures and the elders the voice of many angels, numbering myriads of myriads and thousands of thousands, 12 saying with a loud voice, "Worthy is the Lamb who was slain, to receive power and wealth and wisdom and might and honor and glory and blessing!"

And I heard every creature in heaven and on earth and under the earth and in the sea, and all that is in them, saying, "To him who sits on the throne and to the Lamb be blessing and honor and glory and might forever and ever!"

And the four living creatures said, "Amen!" and the elders fell down and worshiped. Now I watched when the Lamb opened one of the seven seals, and I heard one of the four living creatures say with a voice like thunder, "Come!"

—Revelation 5:1–6:1

The purpose of "Deep Glimpses" is to keep things short and to the point. So I intentionally reduced the amount of exposition in the hope that the reader will take it upon themselves to further investigate, pray, and research points of interest. I am going to keep this as brief and simple as I can. In verse 5 we read: "Weep no more; <u>behold, the Lion of the tribe of Judah</u>, the Root of David, has conquered, so that he can open the scroll and its seven seals."* But from Revelation 5:5 to 6:1, we see the reference to the Lamb.

> 1. I believe the scroll was addressed to the Lamb and contains the attributes being release on the earth that will ultimately combine and transform the Lamb into the Lion.

Jesus came first to the earth as the Lamb of God to take away the sins of the world. But He is returning a second time to execute the wrath of God and to reclaim His realm, which He victoriously won.

> 2. If we are, in fact, the body of Christ, the main reason for the rapture is to gather all the parts of His body back again into the heavens as part of His transformation into the Lion. Our part is bringing to the table the cries for justice and vengeance as do the souls of those under the altar who were martyred.

> 3. It's at this time when Jesus has His whole body gathered again, for the first time in history, in one place and will now conduct the greatest

*emphasis added

and final RE-MEMBERING of His body. At this time, He will hold the concluding resolution of His promise when He lifts the cup—as He said He would not drink of this cup again UNTIL He drinks it anew in His kingdom. Selah.

4. Once His body is fully united with Him (The Head), He then returns with His saints to reclaim the full manifestation of His kingdom on earth. Hallelujah!

Worship God. "For the testimony of Jesus is the spirit of prophecy" (Revelation 19:10).

It's all about Jesus. It's all about His sacrificial death and resurrection. It's all about His victory over Satan, sin, death and the grave . . . All power and authority has been given to Him in Heaven and on the Earth. He said if He is lifted up, He will draw all men unto Himself.

If you recall at the beginning of this booklet, I shared that my wife and I had a time of Communion together. As my wife and I were concluding our Communion time together, we were reflecting on the significant impartation we experienced remembering our salvation, sharing how our walk with Jesus in real time affects our day to day lives, and again coming back to "first love" intimacy with Jesus. Turning to Him again for a fresh touch of His Spirit and renewing our desperate need for Him alone, she mentioned how the three "rememberings" reminded her of John 14:6.

> Jesus said to him, "I am <u>the way,</u> <u>the truth,</u> and <u>the life.</u> No one comes to the Father except through Me."*

If you connect those three aspects of Christ, they align with our three ways of remembering.

The Way = The Cross & Our Salvation

The Truth = Our Consecration or Walking Out Our Faith in Real Time

And the Life = Our Intimacy Where Life Is Continued

Another scripture came to mind as well: It's Hebrews 13:8.

> Jesus Christ is the <u>same yesterday,</u> <u>today,</u> and <u>forever.</u>*

Again, this fits perfectly, as **yesterday** is remembering our wedding or when we first accepted Christ; **today** is remembering we're married and daily walking in His Truth; and **forever** contains the continuation, the procreation of Christ's power to save until we are all gathered before Him and He holds up the cup (as He promised He would) and we all together celebrate our complete redemption with Him Forever. Amen.

Final Reflection

In the opening of this book, I mentioned my Uncle Eddy. Because he was missing his thumb, he was not allowed to hold the bread of Communion in the required and complete

*emphasis added

fashion. I see another message there. What if, because the body of Christ has members missing from it, it cannot function in its complete purpose? What if, because of missing parts, there is a limp or a stumble hindering from becoming everything the world needs it to be?

So can you think of someone who needs to be re-membered? Someone who has been disqualified or severed? If this experience of *remembering* has helped you or someone in your group reconnect to Christ and His body, share this experience with those still left outside His Table.

LEADERS' GUIDE

OPEN

What do you remember when you partake of Communion? Do you remember Jesus died at Calvary 2000 years ago? Do you remember your salvation? What should we be remembering?

Leader: Tonight, we are going to walk through three aspects of "remembering" that apply to our covenant relationship to Christ Jesus.

READ

2 Corinthians 11:2

> *"For I am jealous over you with godly jealousy: for I have espoused you <u>to one husband,</u> that I may present you as a <u>chaste virgin to Christ.</u>"**

Leader: There are many scriptures that connect Christ with His Church, drawing a comparison as with a husband and wife. Another aspect to consider is that our salvation is based upon a covenant just as is marriage. In fact, Jesus states that Communion is the seal of this covenant salvation.

READ

Matthew 26:26–29

> *And as they were eating, Jesus took bread, blessed and broke it, and gave it to the disciples and said, "Take, eat; this is My body." Then He took the cup, and gave thanks, and gave it to them, saying, "Drink from it, all of you. For this is <u>My blood of the new covenant</u>, which is shed for many for the remission of sins. But I say to you, I will not drink of this fruit of the vine from now on until that day when I drink it new with you in My Father's kingdom."**

Leader: We can think of the comparison between biblical marriage and Christ's relationship with us as the Church by envisioning parallel tracks. The first rail is between a husband and wife in marriage, and the second rail is between Christ and His Church (His bride).

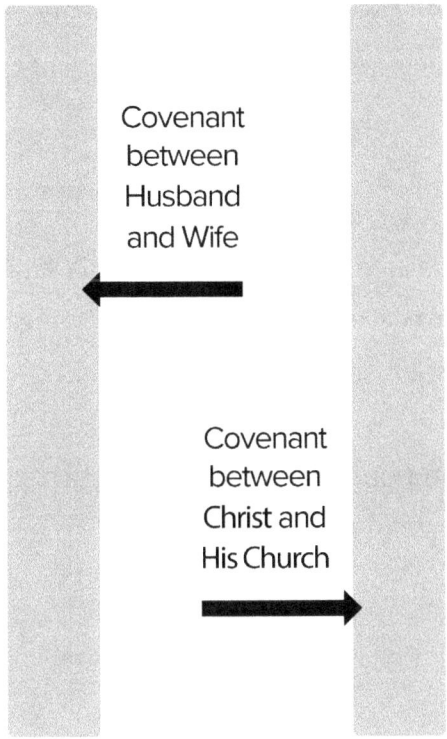

Both relational connections are bound by a covenant. Both involve a sacrifice in the making of that covenant work. Of course, the sacrifice that Christ made was at Calvary's cross where He laid down His life and shed His Blood as the means to ransom His bride from sin, death, and hell. The intrinsic aspects of marriage should be bound by the same level of sacrifice.

There is a reason that traditional marriages took place on an altar—an altar is a place of sacrifice.

Let's first consider the components of remembering as they relate to a marriage. Then, we will apply that same focus as it relates to Christ and our salvation. Using the illustration mentioned earlier, the two lines represent Christ/His Church and marriage. We will start laying horizontal bridges that tie the similar components together. We start by remembering where it all began.

Wedding/Cross

First: REMEMBER YOUR WEDDING—
REMEMBER YOUR SALVATION

Leader: Let's say a married couple was celebrating their anniversary. They go out for a nice dinner, someplace romantic, with candlelight and the right ambiance, and the wife says, "Remember our wedding?" A wedding is a historical event that happened some time ago but can still be remembered. It had specific aspects and experiences that made it unique. The wedding changed your life. From that moment on, you were no longer single, but your life became entwined with another person for better or worse. **And just like you can remember a wedding, so, too, you can remember when your life in Christ began.** Only now you're sitting at the Lord's Table and are asked to remember when you accepted Christ's sacrifice for your sins.

Discuss

- What were the circumstances in your life that brought you to Jesus?
- What did it feel like to be forgiven of your sins?
- When did you make that decision that changed everything for you?

At this time, each person in your group should take turns sharing around the table one's remembrance of when they first gave their life to Jesus Christ.

Second: REMEMBER YOU'RE MARRIED— REMEMBER YOU'RE A CHRISTIAN

Leader: Your life should radically change after you are married. You are no longer a "single" self-serving individual but are now a "plural" entity. The "we" must become stronger than the "I" if you are ever to experience the full expression of being married.

That other person is meant to become your most important focus and priority, but it is so easy to slip back into a self-survival mode. But the exact opposite is what's necessary for a marriage to grow.

The marriage is started at the altar, but it doesn't mean that the sacrifice is over.

READ

1 Corinthians 15:31

> *I affirm, by the boasting in you which I have in Christ Jesus our Lord, I die daily.**

Leader: Imagine you've been married for a while, and your friends call and want to go out. These were the friends that would get you into trouble on occasion, and you can tell they're ready to party. You have a decision to make. That's where you hear a thought in your head say, "Remember, you're married."

Now, I'm not saying that you can never go out with friends, but if you do, you're going out as a married person. Do you see how "remembering" affects your decisions in real time?

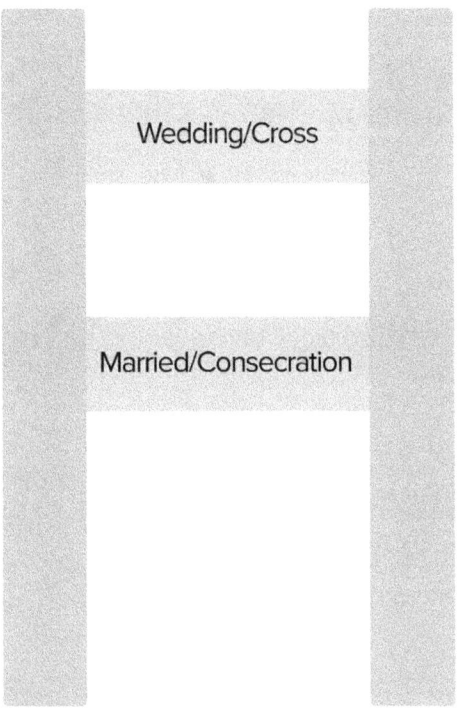

Just like being married affects our decisions and life choices so should our being a Christian apply this same level of remembering to our walk with Christ. Sure, there was a time when you had a real, life-changing encounter with Jesus. But a lot has happened since then. Life happens, and there are many "in your face" realities. There are momentums and shifts, pressures and responsibilities. It is extremely important at those times to "remember you're a follower of Jesus." This should affect the choices you are making in real time today.

I believe remembering is more important
and significant as it should affect
the way we live out our lives.

Discuss

- What kind of correction have you had in your walk with the Lord?
- What things have been cut off because you follow Jesus?
- What positive actions are you doing because of Jesus being in your life?
- How are you living out your faith on a daily basis?

At this time, each group member shares how their current walk (discipleship) or progressive consecration/sanctification with Jesus is affecting current decisions and choices in their lives. Remember, you're a Christian!

Third: REMEMBER YOU'RE IN COMMUNION– REMEMBER YOU'RE IN INTIMACY

Leader: There is an intended exclusive connection for consummating the marriage union where two can become joined together as one. This specific union not only reinstates their priority & exclusivity toward each other but also makes their love increase toward one another and actually makes it possible for new life to enter their union. God made it that way! RE-MEMBER!

This idea of RE-MEMBERING has to be viewed through Scripture as Paul again sheds light onto how we are the body of Christ and each one a member that should connect to other members.

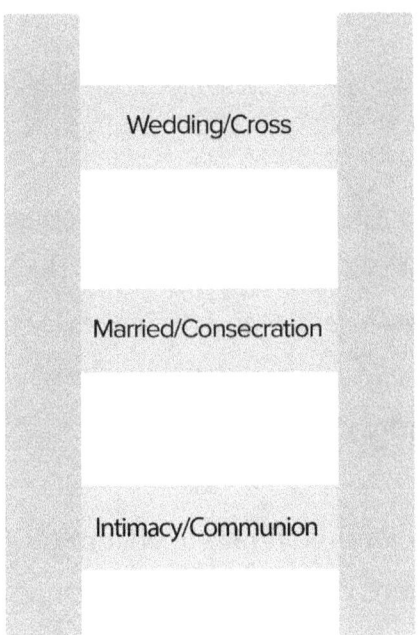

READ

1 Corinthians 12:12

> *For as the body is one and has many members, but all*
> *the members of that one body, being many, are one*
> *body, so also is Christ.*

Communion is meant to illuminate these separating perspectives and bring us all equally to the feet of Jesus. Communion is meant to bring us to a tenderness toward each other, a gentle appreciation and respect in Christ.

READ

Hebrews 10:24–25

> *And let us consider one another in order to stir up*
> *love and good works, not forsaking the assembling*
> *of ourselves together, as is the manner of some, but*
> *exhorting one another, and so much the more as you*
> *see the Day approaching.*

Leader: The goal of this time is to encounter Jesus as if for the first time, intimately. We come to Him confessing our desperate need for Him as if for the first time. Covenant!

We forsake anything that has come between us, any distractions or hindrances to our walk with Him. This is a time of reflection and reverence, a time of prayer. Consecration!

Take a moment to pray and repent if need be or rededicate your life to Him. We are offering ourselves as living sacrifices. Intimacy!

Discuss

- Is there anything you need to confess or lay at the feet of Jesus?
- Is there anything that is separating you from fully committing to your walk with Him?
- In what areas of your life is repentance needed?

DISTRIBUTION OF THE ELEMENTS

READ

Matthew 26:26

> *And as they were eating, Jesus took bread, blessed and broke it, and gave it to the disciples and said, "Take, eat; this is My body."*

Distribute the bread, and everyone partakes.

READ

Matthew 26:27

> *Then He took the cup, and gave thanks, and gave it to them, saying, "Drink from it, all of you. For this is <u>My</u>*

blood of the new covenant, which is shed for many for the remission of sins. But I say to you, I will not drink of this fruit of the vine from now on until that day when I drink it new with you in My Father's kingdom."*

Distribute the wine, and everyone partakes.

End with Prayer

DEEP GLIMPSES SERIES

———·~~·o·e·e·o·K·e·o·o·~~———

Counsel in the heart of man is like deep water,
but a man of understanding will draw it out.
—Proverbs 20:5

———·~~·o·e·e·o·K·o·o·o·~~———

Having served in full-time ministry for over thirty-three years, I have delivered countless sermons and teachings. While many of these messages blur together, a select few stand out as profound revelations—insights that have left an indelible mark on my soul and fundamentally changed my life.

These messages emerged from personal transformative experiences and comprise the books featured here in the Deep Glimpses series.

Remembering Communion
Jesus instructed, "Do this in remembrance of me." As you approach communion, what do you remember? I identified a direct parallel between marriage and communion, noting that the elements we remember about marriage correspond directly to our relationship with Christ and one another. Furthermore, I believe that the Lord's Table should involve more interaction among believers, making the presented pattern inclusive and participative.

The Appliance Gifts

God bestows grace upon each of us, connecting us through gifts that serve the church by strengthening, encouraging, and serving one another. These gifts function much like household appliances, contributing to a healthy and whole spiritual habitation.

The Author of Authority

In addition to being a pastor, I also led worship, fostering a dynamic culture within our worship experiences. However, there came a time when I questioned the direction and purpose of our focus in worship. Worship is far more than mere performance; it is a venue for exchange, impartation, and endowment. Understanding this can profoundly enhance the power in our lives.

Being Effective Between a Rock and a Hard Place

I often felt overwhelmed with ministry tasks such as counseling, leadership meetings, and sermon preparation, while balancing my marriage and family. In desperation, I cried out to the Lord, "I feel like I'm between a rock and a hard place. His response was, "That's where you should be," and He showed me biblical positions to help equip me in making the most of those times.

Lord willing, there will be other books in this series, but for now my prayer is that you will be strengthened and encouraged with these insights and brought into a clearer understanding of your walk with the living God.

www.ingramcontent.com/pod-product-compliance
Lightning Source LLC
Chambersburg PA
CBHW061714120626
46550CB00003B/1213